LEON KIRCHNER

INTERLUDE II

Piano Solo

*Commissioned jointly by the British Broadcasting Corporation
and the Royal Philharmonic Society
as part of their New Generation Artists scheme.*

*The first performance was given by Jonathan Biss
at the City of London Festival on July 1, 2003.*

duration ca. 6 minutes

AMP 8210
First Printing: December 2005

ISBN 0-634-06783-4

Associated Music Publishers, Inc.

DISTRIBUTED BY
HAL•LEONARD®
CORPORATION
7777 W. BLUEMOUND RD. P.O. BOX 13819 MILWAUKEE, WI 53213

for Jonathan Biss

INTERLUDE II

Leon Kirchner

move ahead a little *move ahead a little* *hold back*

Poco meno mosso

move ahead   *poco rit.*

cresc.   *(mf)*   *mp* sub.

poco accel.   *accel.*

ad lib.   *mp*

Tempo I ♩. = 88   **Presto**

mf sf   *f sf*

più mosso   *hold back*   *move ahead*

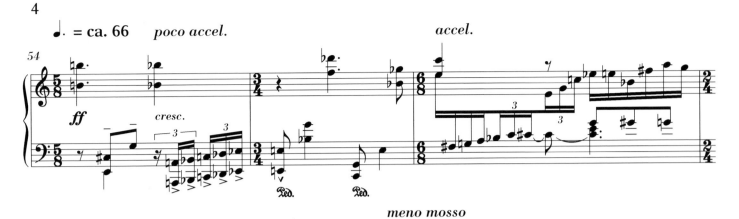

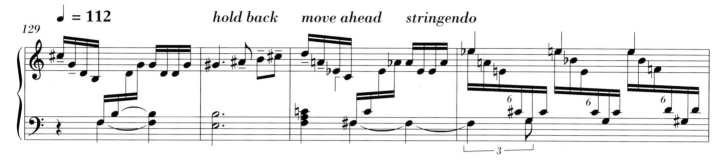

hold back   *move ahead*   *stringendo*